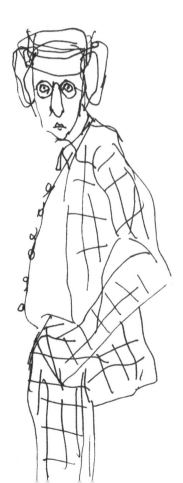

BIS Publishers

Building Het Sieraad, Postjesweg 1, 1057 DT Amsterdam
The Netherlands

T +31 (0)20 515 02 30 | bis@bispublishers.com
www.bispublishers.com

ISBN-13: 978-9063694838

Copyright © 2018 Nimrod Kamer (text),
Isabella Cotier (illustrations) and BIS Publishers.

Art direction & Design:
Charlie Behrens (studio-behrens.com)

The Social Climber's Handbook

A Shameless Guide by
NIMROD KAMER

My name is Nimrod...

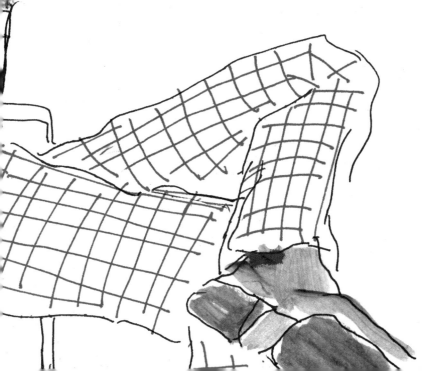

...and I'm a retired underachiever

Social climbing isn't crass or rude in my view, it's a form of class warfare; a redistribution of likes.

Recent graduates should realise by now that their alma doesn't matter. Skills will get you nowhere.

Machines are taking all the jobs and robbing social workers from fulfilling their social mobility goals.

The parasitic elites are sucking up the world's wealth and you should suck back up by any means.

My relentless presence in members clubs, royal galas, award ceremonies and private islands is a constant reminder to the top 0.1% that their accomplishments are infinitely more banal than my failures.

This book will teach you how to sneak into red and purple carpets, invoice celebrities for services not rendered, cheat your way to social media stardom and be present at every shindig you weren't invited to. You will find these words true, sad, sad but true, or just sad enough to be true yet somehow still false.

A lifelong wannabe will never be a has-been.

Friends come and go – blocked people are forever.

Unfollow your dreams.

Nimrod: I changed your Wikipedia page again.

Kanye: Why?

Nimrod: I'll change it back for 0.02 bitcoins.

Kanye: [to bodyguard] Take this guy's number — he knows how to work Wikipedia.

Nimrod: I bought fake Youtube dislikes for your trailer.

Ed Norton: —

[conversation over]

Remember these five guidelines:

1

Better ask for forgiveness than permission.

2

If you got them by the balls – their hearts and minds will follow.

3

You were called worse things by better people.

4

Hope = Potential gain divided by probability.

5

God is debt.

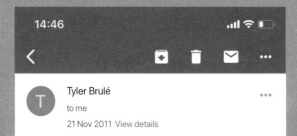

14:46

Tyler Brulé
to me
21 Nov 2011 View details

Dear Nimrod,

I've spoken to many of our editors and all seem to have been contacted by you. If they haven't come back to you then it's due to the fact they're not keen on your stories.

Kind regards.

1st rejection email

investigating Chiltern Firehouse (London) with a sunbed & a hose

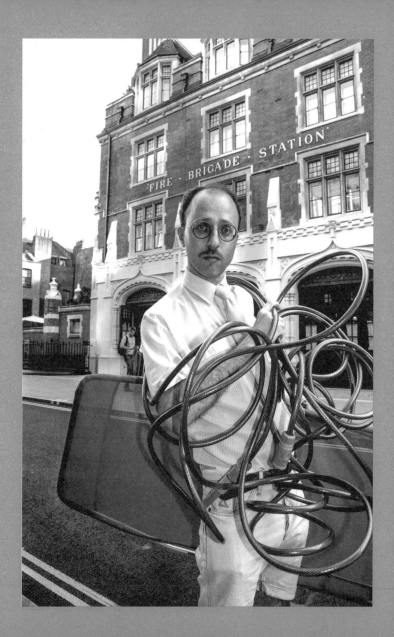

WALK IN BACKWARDS

Guest lists are hard to overcome. The doorman can see your face.

They will eject you faster than you can say 'Jack Guinness'. Wait for a moment of disarray at reception and quickly moonwalk inside, smooth, like MJ, no one will notice you. Some may assume you're coming back in reverse from the smoking area.

Don't look ahead until you are in.

Turn your face forward - you lose. Carry on moving backwards and hit the bar. Slam your back on it. Order a drink without looking. When the drink arrives glance up and say thank you. If you hold a drink you're safe. Keep your JOMO going — joy of missing out.

TILL DEBT
DO US PART

#flaccid   #lit

Members clubs have a soft spot for those who owe them money. Arrive in the morning with $250 in cash and demand entry to pay your bill from last night. There is no bill. You then insist, it's at the bar upstairs.

**Last night was tumultuous.
Tinder is the night.
God is debt.**

When you're upstairs keep on looking for your tab. Order sparkling water and allow them to check everywhere, no rush. On your way out leave a scarf in the cloakroom permanently. Use the cloakroom ticket to get in the following day. Now you're pretty much a member. Start talking to various other members and offer them your services, such as Wikipedia editing and iCloud tips.

LOOK LIKE
A BUILDER

Arrive in a hi-viz jacket and an ear-piece. Lean down and talk to the ear-piece constantly. Walk in swiftly. Come out. Walk in again. Make yourself a three part suit made of the high-vis jacket material. Cycle in. Put your helmet and bicycle in the cloakroom.

Fluorescent is the new Velour.

If you're at the gala to fix the air conditioning you'll always be needed. Tell party goers about your profession. Your life has been full of terrible misfortunes most of which never happened. Lend yourself to others. A wise person sees as much as he ought to, not as much as he can.

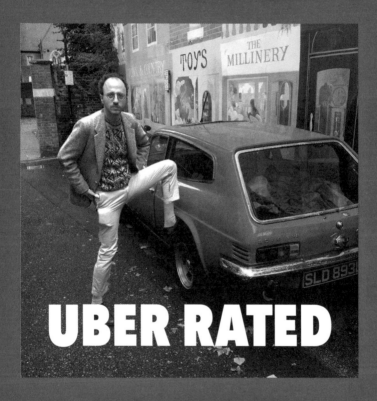

nnimrodd
Hackney Central London Overground Station ›

•••• vodafone UK 4G   12:56

FARE ESTIMATE   ✕

Hackney Central
United Kingdom

Tehran

——— EXEC ———

£7,960-10,613

Fares may vary due to traffic, weather, and other factors.
Estimate does not include discounts or promotions.

Liked by **henryhudson_bk**, **abbyow** and **102 others**

nnimrodd My @uber trip to Tehran

View all 23 comments

1 APRIL 2015

Man goes on journey to become Uber's worst passenger and films the confused reaction of drivers when he asks to be scored just one star

By Alexandra Klausner for MailOnline
06:01, 03 Dec 2014, updated 09:52, 03 Dec 2014

◉ +7

Meet beautiful strangers randomly at the back seat of an UberPOOL and marry them.

Uber is the new Tinder.

Split the Uber fare with long lost friends on your phone's contact list. They aren't in the car with you – it makes no difference. Some might be ignorant enough to pay, tapping 'accept' by mistake. Uber allows you to share the cost with up to four people...

Find rich friends on your contact list and split the fare with them. They do not need to be in the car.

Some might be ignorant enough to accept. Your journey will never be boring again.

WEDDING CRASH

Penetrate any wedding if you have more than 20 mutual friends with the bride or groom. Present your social media accounts at the door. Show how much you have liked the couple's posts over the years. Do not require a table, just a chair by the altar.

When inside hit the dancefloor the hardest. If asked which side you're on, return the question and say you're from the opposite side.

After five hours retire to the lavatory, leaving the booth's door unlocked, so no one suspects you're there. Just like on a train.

FAKE NEWS*

*before it was a thing (circa 2012)

od at the Gavin McInnes Show

od at the Gavin McInnes Show

Surveillance paradise: How one man spied on NSA in Bahamas (VIDEO)

Published time: 2 Aug, 2014 18:26
Edited time: 3 Aug, 2014 07:28

Video still from RT video / RT

video report following Edward Snowden's leaked documents showing all Bahamian phones are being taped by the US

How I Faked Obama's Kenyan Birth

I am Nimrod Kamer, aka Peter Rehnquist, the creator of the "real" 'Obama Kenya Birth 2012' film. I am happy to present to you the behind-the-scenes making-of footage of the birthing-video hoax.

📷 1 ↗

The fakest fake video in the faking world.

Share 📘   **Tweet** 🐦

A prank on Donald Trump, who in 2012 offered $5M to anyone who will provide him with "proof" that Obama was born in Kenya

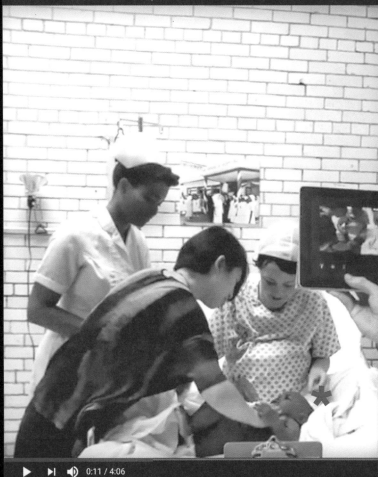

▶ ▶| 🔊 0:11 / 4:06

*Baby hired from Craigslist

CLICK
FARMERS

Buy fake followers, fake comments, fake likes, fake dislikes (on Youtube).

You'll create much needed employment in Bangladesh.

Most click farms are located in Asia. Why pay Facebook for an ad to promote your content when you can pay directly to farmers?

Most of your real friends are fake people, so what's the difference?

Drop 1,000 followers on your loved ones account for Christmas.

PRESS YOUR
CREDENTIALS

Live and eat out of PR gift bags. If you need more dog food: email a dog food PR company and ask to write about their dog food. They'll send you loads. If you need a place to stay try living in a sample flat to save rent. Sample flats are a façade of a flat in a newly built luxury apartment bloc. The coffee machine doesn't really work and walls are made of wallpaper. Ethically you better not write about these products without declaring your writing is sponsored.

It is okay to disappoint PR companies and not deliver on the writeup.

The entire PR business is based on false promises.

MINUS ONE

... on the guest list

Throw your own socal media party. Put everyone on the guest list as their name and add:

minus 1, minus 2, minus 3.

When a −1 guest arrives, another guest needs to leave. This will create healthy tension and chaos at the door.

Guests need to show their Instagram profile at the door to prove they have more followers than pictures.

Ratios matter. If guests have posted too many pictures they need to stand aside and delete some, then try again.

Make the inside look like a street. Tell the DJ to play car ambience.

Usher everyone in so they can queue to leave.

IGNORE MY PREVIOUS EMAIL

No one will read your emails.

Unless — you send another email asking them to ignore your previous email. Then they'll think you acciden- tally sent something important and read it immediately. They may even open an attachment. As a rule avoid sending attachments unless it's an invoice. Write

[//]

in the subject line on all emails. If a recipient knows what an email is about from it's subject line - you failed. The best first impressions are misleading. Have the word "Done" on your e-signature. Always check the spam folder before checking your inbox. Make a book- mark of it.

Socks for Lily Allen

FASHION FROW-UP*

*frow = front row

Notable guests have their names printed on the bench at the front row. Sit next to a name you fancy. When the show is about to begin you'd be asked to move. Refuse. Say there's no time for you to move, because "the show is about to begin".

Talk to the person you chose to sit next to, mistaking them for a different famous individual.

Name-flopping is much more powerful than Namedropping.

When you get a name wrong it's a conversation upper, mixed with an element of shock.

Wear pink Crocs and stretch your legs forward, trespassing the runway. Hold scoreboards with numbers. Rate the outfits 5.7, 7.5, 8.4 just like in the Olympics. When the show ends go to where the models came from and crash the backstage area.

PITCH IN

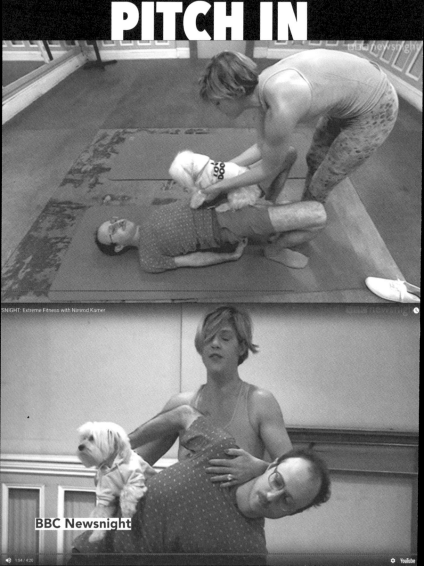

SNIGHT: Extreme Fitness with Nimrod Kamer

BBC Newsnight

1:54 / 4:20   YouTube

You are inside the BBC building, for whatever reason.

Don't leave.

Stay in. Walk between the departments and pitch your story ideas to each one — sports, news, drama etc. If anyone wonders why you're still there, say you're between meetings. When things get heated go to the staff canteen and join a table.

Express your views on what they're talking about, with solutions, like more poetry mixed with bitcoins.

Complain about the food like they do. Complain about upper management. Get a desk at one of the open spaces and request a temp email address. Past midnight you may be allowed to stay another day.

HOTEL
HIATUS

Book an Airbnb opposite the hotel in which the party is at. Arrive in a bathing suit and towel. Dress codes do not apply to hotel guests. Check on Instagram: who's sitting next you in the lobby or pool.

Do a location search to see who posted a pic at the venue. Approach them and offer your services.

Ask the concierge to print some plane tickets and a 150 page manuscript.

PDF your way in.

High-end locations offer these services to anyone. They're happy to provide umbrellas, pens and towels. When asked for your room number say you checked out 5 minutes ago.

Espresso = unlimited cookies.

CREATE A
TED TALK

A CV is never complete without a TED Talk...

Create a stage with T, E & D letters alongside a round red carpet.

Film it. Cut the video with audience reactions from real TED Talks. Release it on all social medias thanking TED for the opportunity. People pay £5K to be in a TED audience and mingle with Al Gore. You should be humble to have been given the chance to express yourself. Doesn't matter what you talk about. Read a play or play a tool. Mention 'paradigm shift' and 'plagiarise shift' twice, then do a dance move and collapse.

[applause].

Nimrod's fake TED on how to monetise Wikipedia

WHERE TO LIVE?

Choose a city to live in only if it has the following services:

    1) Uber
    2) Soho House
    3) VICE magazine office

example:

**Istanbul has all three.
Tel Aviv has none.**

SMOKING AREA

Every party has a smoking section outside. Entering it is much easier than entering the party...

Arrive without a coat. Put one leg over the barrier and slip in holding a cigarette.

Don't actually smoke.

Talk to people. Follow some inside pretending you know them.

Fake a cough.

Lawrence Van Hagen's apartment

GETTY
IMAGES

gettyimages®
Dan Kitwood

Nimrod and Rebekah Brooks
outside the supreme court

Get to know all the Getty photographers in your area by name.

Do not get too close to them. They must be at an appropriate distance to take a picture. One cannot take a picture while hugging. The morning after — wake up at 6am and call Getty.

Make sure your name is spelled correctly

If you got caught in the background of someone else's picture they may tag you as 'Guest'. Show up at the Getty offices. Getty will last a lot longer than Facebook. For centuries to come it will become the historic record of your social work.

Many Getty returns.

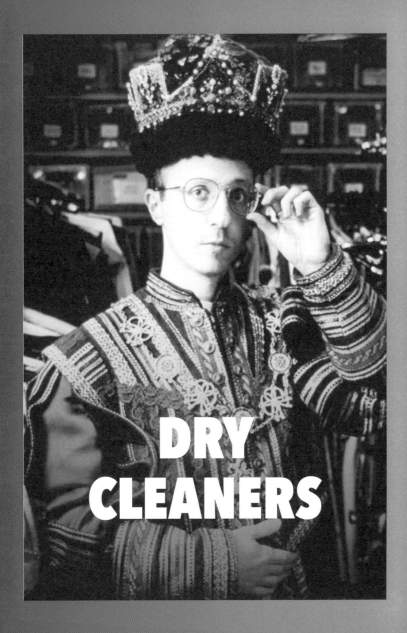

DRY
CLEANERS

Leave half your wardrobe at various dry cleaners around town. This will double your closet space. Buy more outfits and leave them in hotels and members clubs.

A cloakroom ticket is better than a membership.
A cloakroom ticket lasts a lifetime.

(See 'Till Debt Do Us Part').

INTERVIEW
YOUR BOSS

Don't try to be interviewed for a job. Rather, interview your future employer instead for your fake publication. No one enjoys interviewing candidates, yet everyone enjoys being interviewed for a magazine themselves.

Become friends with the boss, then get the job.

Never suck up to your future employer: suck down.

UNFOLLOW
YOUR HEART

Take social media offline — to the streets. Talk like you tweet. Run into a famous person and say:

" I unfollowed you. "

They'll be intrigued you bothered reading their posts in the first place. Quote their recent tweets out loud and explain what made you stop following.

Everyone loves discussing their tweets, as opposed to their career. Promise to follow back if they work harder on their online persona.

See how it goes.

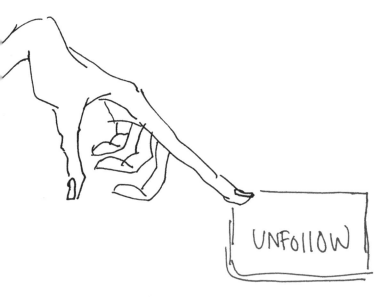

The tweet:

Derek Blasberg
@DerekBlasberg

I didn't think I could love Thailand as much as I do right now in this moment.

Nimrod Kämer
@nnimrodd

Sorry for unfollowing, @DerekBlasberg

The DM:

Derek Blasberg

Derek Blasberg
To unfollow is one thing, to verbalize it to the person is another. The world needs less people like you.

Nimrod Kämer
I couldn't swallow the Thailand tweet..

Unfollowing in a non public manner is even more offensive

Derek Blasberg was described by Gawker as the "greediest man in fashion".

73

Jenny Eclair @jennyeclair · 39m

How horrible the world is this week

Nimrod Kamer @nnimrodd · 30m

Sorry for unfollowing, @jennyeclair

Jenny Eclair ✓
@jennyeclair

@nnimrodd sorry for not giving a flying fuck

16/12/2014 11:57

**Jenny Eclair is an English comedian,
played in Grumpy Old Women between
2004 and 2007**

FKA Nimrod ✓
@nnimrodd

Sorry for unfollowing, @jonronson

11/02/2015 19:34

📊 VIEW TWEET ACTIVITY

↩   ⇄   ★   •••

jonronson @jonronson   2m
@nnimrodd that's fine - thanks so
much for alerting me.

jonronson @jonronson   44s
@nnimrodd weird for someone in
your position to be so passive
aggressive tho

Jon Ronson writes about online shaming

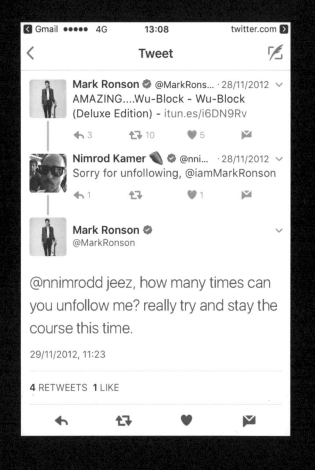

Tweet

Mark Ronson ✔ @MarkRons... · 28/11/2012 ⌄
AMAZING....Wu-Block - Wu-Block
(Deluxe Edition) - itun.es/i6DN9Rv

↩ 3   ⟲ 10   ♥ 5   ✉

Nimrod Kamer 🍃 ✔ @nni... · 28/11/2012 ⌄
Sorry for unfollowing, @iamMarkRonson

↩ 1   ⟲   ♥ 1   ✉

Mark Ronson ✔   ⌄
@MarkRonson

@nnimrodd jeez, how many times can
you unfollow me? really try and stay the
course this time.

29/11/2012, 11:23

4 RETWEETS **1** LIKE

↩   ⟲   ♥   ✉

Mark Ronson is a DJ in Tel Aviv

ollowing celebs. Alexa, Pixie, Kate, Kitty

Direct Message   >

Share My Info   >

Unfollowing kittybrucknell...

View L   >

Unfollow   Block

kittybrucknell does not follow nnimrodd

Report as Spam

ollowing celebs. Alexa, Pixie, Kate, Kitty

SOCIAL
DIET

Wake up as late as possible to save money. 1pm at a minimum, everyday. You will only need to eat a croissant and one meal as the evening approaches.

9 to 5 people become obese because they have to eat 3 meals a day.

Working in an open spaces is filthy. It will make you sick.

Hibernate your way to the future.

Sleep more.

DEFLECT
DENY
DENOUNCE

Never answer direct questions and always deny things you weren't asked about.

Instead of asking "What is your salary?" Say "Everyone knows you make $100K"

...and let the other person confirm or deny it.

If someone got hurt use an if-apology or a non-apology apology.

Say you feel bad for your friend's tears, without mentioning your wrong-doings. If asked to bring wine to a party say "Yes, I'll pass by the wine shop on my way". It doesn't mean you plan to buy any.

Bill Clinton's bodyguard admires Nimrod's suit

APPROACH YOUR LEADER

Pretend to take selfies with corrupt members of parliament, ministers and lobbyists — but take a video instead.

#MOFIE

 **INDEPENDENT** ☰

News › UK › UK Politics

EU citizen confronts Theresa May telling her: 'I'm about to get deported'

Romanian passport holder approaches Prime Minister at exclusive summer party

Independent Staff | Friday 14 July 2017 15:45 BST |
💬 133 comments

 **1K**
shares

👍 **Like**   Click to follow
Indy Politics

NK: Hey, I'm Nimrod, Can we get a picture? I'm a Romanian passport holder and I'm about to get deported.

TM: No you're not, you've got the Citizen's Rights paper

NK: You said it, you said it — but that's not the same as what you originally offered.

TM: It's very similar. The key difference is the European Courts of Justice

NK: Well, I'm still worried.

TM: Well, you shouldn't be worried

FN: [Fraser Nelson, editor of the Spectator]: Everything's going to be fine, I think — you needn't worry

Nigel Farage and Rupert Murdoch celebrating Brexit

Nimrod raising money for a new yacht
for the queen, endorsed by then justice
minister Michael Gove

Make oligarchs spend an excruciating amount of time posing for you. Interrogate them about tax avoidance in the meanwhile. Gonzo Journalism.

If you are not invited to a party you are under no obligation to behave.

Work for the many (your online audience), not the few. Phew. Don't try to please soirée people just because they seem lavish.

The whole point of a democracy is the right to confront politicians in an awkward manner carrying a camera and a stick.

SHARE YOUR RECEIPTS

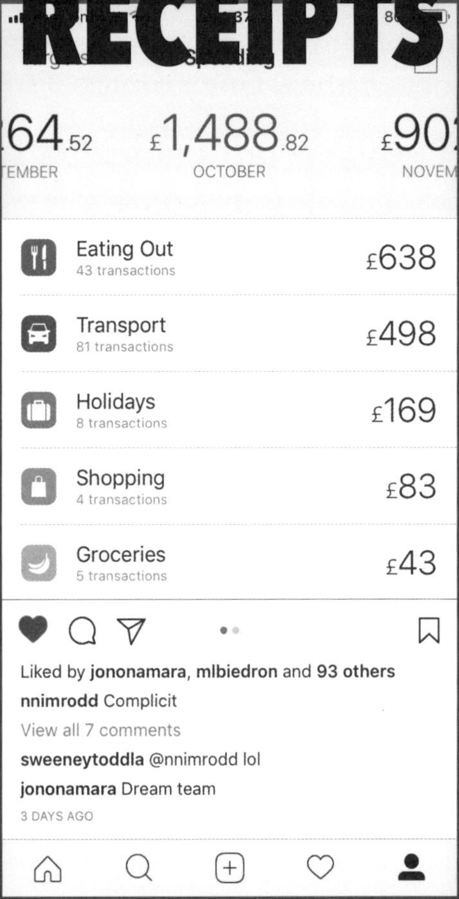

The happiness effect. Everyone is posting sexy pictures relentlessly. Your body is your battleground. Your followers know every trench.

Being naked online isn't risky anymore.

Posting your finances is the only taboo left.

Be brave and share all your receipts on Instagram.

Don't post a picture by without showing the price, or the mental toll.

Share all of your bills, overdraft and mortgage on Twitter.

ART
RUZZLE

Auction your ego.

ART & DESIGN | October 12, 2015

An Idiot's Guide to Buying Art at Frieze

We're not saying our author is an idiot,
we're just not accepting any responsibility
for the advice stated here

Written by **NIMROD KAMER**

Go to every art fair around the world. Hong Kong, Miami, Basel. You're a collector, not a journalist. Arrive with a canvas of your own to make the impression that you just bought it.

No one is allowed to take their purchases home. Except you.

Go into the UBS bank lounge using someone else's guest pass. VIPs can get unlimited guest passes if they claim to have lost them. Ask to rent art rather than buy it.

Art = Property.

Get a vault in Switzerland for tax purposes. Art is a commodity made of money. Some canvases have cash inside them.

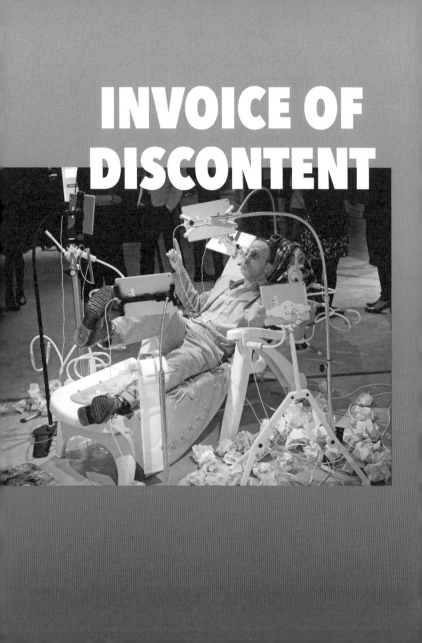

Send payment requests to everyone, all the time. When dealing with big corporations like VICE Magazine — submit the same invoice three times. Once by fax, once as a JPG, once by hand delivery.

You might get paid more than once by accident.

Add an agony-fee for the misery of drafting the invoice to the invoice. First as tragedy, then as farce, then as modus operandi.

Invoice wealthy friends constantly for any favor you've ever done them.

Giving Pearce Brosnan his fake sextape

NAME ONLY

Nimrod Kamer

Business cards should contain your name only.

- No email
- No website
- No address
- No phone.

Nobody's gonna call you. Finding you should be an online escapade.

When you've handed over your business card, pull out a pair of scissors and cut it in two.

Keep the surname. Give away the first name. A name remembered is a job done. Anyone can direct message you. Carpe DM.

SNEAKPEAK

Eventually you will get invited to places legitimately.

Don't forget the little people.

Allow young social climbers to use your name at the door. You will get in anyway. Give out your press pass as you exit an event. Allow fans to re-attach your wristband. Teach them how to use a high-vis jacket to pretend they're builders. Invite them to the pool in Hôtel du Cap-Eden-Roc if you're already in.

A healthy society is built on generosity and ladders. Social mobility.

Your façade is their façade.

THROWAWAY TICKETING

Never fly from London to New York. Fly from Dublin to New York via London.

Every city has its hidden city.

For the US, it's Dublin. For Asia, it's Amsterdam. A business class ticket from Amsterdam back to London and then to Hong Kong costs less than an Premium Economy ticket from London to Hong Kong.

The first leg of a journey must not be skipped.

On your way back from Hong Kong to Amsterdam you may throwaway the last leg of the ticket and get out in London.

Count your air miles every day.

DATING

Quiche

Procrasturbate

Olympic medalist Louise Hazel

Be in a power couple.

Have mutual frenemies.

For romance's sake – fly separately, meet at the destination. Don't share links with each other to pass the time – only original content. Use google images for sexy pics in case you get hacked. No nudes is good nudes.

Resist everything except temptation.

When dating rich kids always say you're a marxist at their family dinners.

The key to dating is 10 metre long phone-charging cables that reach your bed.

Every morning tell your spouse:

"I misunderestimated you."

with Alex Karpovsky (GIRLS)

[MORE]
REJECTION

with Zosia Mamet (GIRLS)

---------- Forwarded message ----------

On Nov 12, 2014, at 10:46 AM, Nimrod
Kamer <nnimrodd@gmail.com> wrote:

> On a diferent note - I'd love to
> interview the cast of GIRLS, or
> just Alex Karpovsky if everyone
> else is busy, for a bbc news
> featurette.

From: **Audrey Gelman**
<▮▮▮▮▮▮▮▮▮▮▮▮▮▮▮▮>
Date: Wednesday, November 12, 2014
Subject: Corrections to your story on Lena's
PP Shirt - timely
To: Nimrod Kamer <nnimrodd@gmail.com>,
Rob Price <▮▮▮▮▮▮▮▮▮▮▮>

Thanks Nimrod and off the record again, I'll
be advising the cast of GIRLS to not to talk
to you.

Audrey

email to GIRLS HBO agent

#YODA – You only die alone

#Gravie – a cemetary selfie

Nimrod's films and journalism made in collaboration with

William Pine // Heydon Prowse // Tom Bell

Henry Hudson // Jono Namara // Joe Wade
Karley Sciortino // Samantha King
Paige Elkington // Andre Balazs

Emilie McMeekan // Dylan Jones // Alex Miller
Andy Capper // Jason Lester // Dylan Jones

Billie JD Porter // Fee Craig // Rocco Castoro

Joe Wade // Nikolay Bogachihin

Bill Prince // Ian Katz // Takashi Murakami

Big shout to **Hannah Ghorashi**
@iknowyouthatsmypurse